DOMINIE READERS

The Changing Chameleon

Story by Janie Spaht Gill, Ph.D.
Illustrations by Bob Reese

DOMINIE PRESS
Pearson Learning Group

Tina and Terri took a walk
toward the park one day.

3

Then Tina saw a chameleon sunning as they walked along the way.

Look, a chameleon," Tina said.
erri asked her, "Where?"
In the grass," said Tina.

So they ran very hurriedly, but...

the chameleon wasn't there.

"There he is," said Tina.
Terri asked her, "Where?"
"In the leaves," said Tina.

So they crept very slowly, but...

the chameleon wasn't there.

"I see him once again,"
said Tina.
Terri asked her, "Where?"
"On the tree bark," Tina said.

15

So they tiptoed
very lightly, but...
the chameleon wasn't there.

"He's jumped again," said Tina.
Terri asked her, "Where?"
"Into the flowers," Tina said.
So they crawled very softly, but..

the
chameleon
wasn't
there.

Tina said, "That chameleon's much too tricky.
Let's head back to the house."

They never knew the
chameleon sat...
on the back of Terri's blouse!

Curriculum Extension Activities

The Changing Chameleon

■ Have the children create a chameleon puppet out of white socks. They could then dramatize the chameleon's route as he moved from place to place. Other places where the chameleon could have hidden may be added to the dramatization.

■ Have the children make a large chameleon costume for all of them to get under. They can make the costume out of white butcher paper, and color it using markers. Two small holes cut in the front could serve as the chameleon's eyes. Use cardboard handles to attach to the inside for the children to hold.

■ Have the children create a park mural and color in various things they might see in a park: trees, grass, bushes, trails, slides, swings, bars, tennis courts, etc. Then draw chameleons hiding in various places.

About the Author

Dr. Janie Spaht Gill brings twenty-five years of teaching experience to her books for yo children. During her career thus far, she has taught at every grade level, from kindergarten thro college. Gill has a Ph.D. in reading education, with a minor in creative writing. She is curre residing in Lafayette, Louisiana with her husband, Richard. Her fresh, humorous topics are insp by the things her students say in the classroom. Gill was voted the 1999-2000 Louisiana Elemen Teacher of the Year for her outstanding work in primary education.

Softcover Edition ISBN 0-7685-2164-5
Library Bound Edition ISBN 0-7685-2472-5

Printed in Singapore
4 5 6 7 8 9 10   10 09 08 07

Dominie
Press

Pearson Learning Group

1-800-321-3106
www.pearsonlearning.com